In the name of God, the Most Gracious, the Most Merciful

To Him We All Return

(Poems)
Anand Ahmad Ali Salih

Preface

Eternally grateful for the path of submission, Islam, these are my thoughts and wishes as I continue to walk towards the garden of the beautiful surrender. I hope that you are accommodating of my mistakes and flaws, and I pray that we meet in Jannah by the mercy of our Lord.

- Anand Ahmad Ali Salih
anandahmadalisalih@gmail.com
anandmur@buffalo.edu

Contents

Part 1: Dearest Palestine

1. If my heart could

If my heart could hold a drop from the sea of love
you poured into the heart of your beloved messenger,
I could carry a smile that I belong to his nation, O Lord.
What could I possibly be proud to tell him about this world
where his beloved souls left to be trampled under boots,
except that I tried to carry prayers for them tonight?

If my heart, before the sea of his tear drops for this nation,
could shed a drop seeking stations for the innocent littles,
I could carry a smile that I belong to his nation, O Lord.
What could I possibly carry for him in my soul, from this world
where children were left to starve and feasts locked away,
except my requests to be forgiven for being among heartless?

If my soul, by the sea of courage that filled his voice,
could scream that neglect and ignorance are the gravest of mirk,
I could carry a smile that I belong to his nation, O Lord.
What could I possibly show him from my deeds in this world
where the mothers were left on streets to cry for their children's lives,
except that I watched helplessly as the kings decided to silence them?

---

2. Court of Absolute Justice

O spineless rulers of the richest barrens,
don't you tremble at night in fear? for each -
of us pray every night to be a witness against you
in the court of absolute justice. We pray we never -
forget how you guided the cannibal demons to little children,
with your silence, for you were promised mountains of gold.

What would be the colour of nations you build,
as your hands are soaked in blood of innocent littles,
what would be the pride of your children?
when all you have accomplished is aiding the dark
to burn angels alive for gifts of golden arrows and wine?

What would be colour of your shame on the day
you would stand before Lord of all worlds and lights
to answer for the greatest sin to accomplish on earth?

What would be the nightmares of your senility and death
when all you have accomplished is to remain in your palace
while little limbs are pulled and faces are burned,
as you strip yourself in the high of shining trinkets from hell?

---

3. Slaves by Choice

We are the slaves by choice to the evil lands who
swarm against you for being the sparks of truth.
We are the silence by choice to the torture
the flying demons and stinking zombies
afflict to your beautiful little ones, O Palestine.

We are the greed by ignorance for comfort we earn,
when you bleed and starve in the gaols of dark
when you sleep hoping we would come to save you
forgive us for being cowards that chain themselves,
forgive us for being blind when your kids are murdered.

With pangs of hunger you leave this world.
With our affluence we failed you, each of us -
clinging to the threads of slavery for grains,
forgetting the only source of sustenance
is with you, by you and always loves you.

---

4. Forgive me

O the little lights of life erased by rains of fire, forgive me
for being from the world who thinks they are killing rats.
I see no rats no devils struck, just fragrant blossoms
who would have smiled if they were left to live.

Forgive me for being of the world
who said lives will be lost in battles,
for being of the generation,
who said you don't matter since you own no things.

Who does own even a thing in this garden -
we came to share a dream in our roles?
Forgive me for not praying for you enough.
I wish you could come tell me in the next,
of the angels and heavens who welcomed you back.

O the little lights of life whose limbs and eyes -
are snatched away in the endless race for power,
I wish I knew what you want of me, should I be louder
or should I pray till this body of mine decays?

---

5. Fragrance of Palestine

Forgive us, for we were silent when
your fragrances were erased
in the name of futile revenge,
witness were we and will be,
O those juvenile blooms of this soil,
this world might forget you too.

When on the day when each sand grain
would bear witness against the rulers
and the tongues that stood against you,
may my soul laugh in ecstasy as
each of your heads be crowned,
O the little dreams that were too pure
for this world we build.

---

6. Contracts of wealth

O souls murdered on contracts of west of wealth,
I wish we had hearts soft enough to pray more,
for we remain witness to the play of vanishing promises,
why do they think sleep is sweet on stolen beds?

O souls mocked by the laughs of powers of world,
I wish we had tears for little souls that cry for help,
for we remain silent before the scripts of greed,
and the world may forget the act of denied rights.

O souls painted as demons on skies of the foolish,
I wish we had souls of human enough to be loud,
for we hope tree of peace to sprout in their hard hearts,
as if we can ever redraw the smiles of your lost lives.

---

7. Isolated Stars

O stars isolated in the crowds for you stand for truth,
shine brighter in loneliness, for the world chose darkness,
shine with every bead of compassion blessed in heart,
for your shine is your gratitude to the creator of all lights,
may each moment pull your hearts to surrender absolute.

O lips who carry prayers for the oppressed souls
even in the darkest nights of the coldest of winters,
your prayers only to the Lord of seven skies,
even when world's colours change with seasons -
may yours stay ever for truth, in darkness and at noon.

O voices lost among the thunders of deafening ignorance,
keep speaking, for you are not of this world, but merely
penniless travellers to this land, holding onto just the truth
even as storms pass by and nights prolong without cease,
let's pray we are forgiven for we couldn't do enough.

---

8. Most Beautiful of Lands

Wonder how luminous does your sky look,
O the most beautiful of lands,
as thousand beings of light await
to welcome back the bright souls
from the world they were murdered?

How brightly they would appear
on the day when we would be judged,
would I be allowed to at least see
when innocence would be honoured,
O the land of the strongest faith?

When I am brought back from my grave
to your land, could I see in awe your men,
who had to bury their innocent kids
because the world was too blind to help,
as the merchants of hell let loose terror?

Forgive us for not loving you enough,
we ask forgiveness of not being human,
of swallowing news that mock you,
of not being loud enough to get you help.
O dearest of lands, may you be honoured.

---

9. What does it mean

What does having ambition mean to this traveller,
when the body breathes from the world each step,
but the heart sad to be among the greediest of people?
What does having chance to pray mean to a believer,
than to spend every chance to ask for the truth's victory,
when the tyrants rule to sacrifice lives throughout the world?

What does being alive mean to this inhabitant of earth, O Lord,
when infants starve while powers still force us debate for them,
but to love those little ones wishing they be fed and healed?
What does having chance to write about them mean to this self,
than to pray for your blessing to heal every child and oppressed?

Part 2: The Surrender

10. When you alone will remain

Am I the flute that got carved in the form so beautiful,
to sing your praise and left in time to wait in this crowd?
Am I the music that you blessed me to be, Ya Rabb,
to be your love and cover this room in a huge hug of bliss?
Am I this breath, of divine intimacy, that is eternally indebted
for its existence for it knows nothing but your love?

Am I the tune which keeps forgetting about its Lord
and wandering in melodies in search for happiness never there?
Am I the tear drop that shed from this heart, in moments
I realize I am nothing but a drop from the infinite mercy?
Am I a drop or a am I a bubble in this ocean, Ya Allah,
or just a wish to be me, whatever you want me to be?

When the time stops, colours vanish and forms dissolve completely,
when you alone will remain, O the Lord of all forms and beings,
can you forgive me for not knowing enough to be your true slave,
for I am but a forgetful child lost in crowds of dancing emotions?

---

11. When I die

At the start of the path, when I die, will I be afraid,
at the start of the day when the moon leaves, do I cease?
When the entirety that I can ever know is single drop of you mercy,
where in this creation is that I am alone when I am forever loved?
Where a still mind and an awake seeker meet, I am still in search,
where in this journey do I think I can meet, when I haven't started?

Inside the trembles of fear that shake a seeker's heart,
is always the gem of hope that never ceases to give another chance.
Would I be ok in moments time when I would leave the familiar,
free from the cage that I have grown fond of ignorance in mind?
Would I be ever alone even in the ungrateful nights I spend in sleep,
for you are the ever forgiveness that lets my existence be out of love?

If I in vain scream for help when I leave this cage,
would I be reminded that I have never belonged in crowds.
I am a seeker lost in heart to the thirst of love beyond worlds,
would I be reminded that I am nothing but a speck of arrogance
that travelled the seas in oblivion of whose canvas in I seek?
When I meet death of this world, would I smile for I finally start?

If even a word of my repenting body is of true, would I
end up ever-thirsty, for you are the benevolent giver,
all paths of world and heavens are yours to guide us in,
merely because we are ungrateful but you are forgiving.
Would I know the truth of love towards you, O Lord,
such that my heart ceases being for itself but for you?

---

12. Nothing remains but the Lord

Ripples who thought they're everything to the pond,
gave themselves each a name to treasure their time,
overjoyed by each's arrival and saddened by each's demise,
each ripple did think pond was theirs to inherit,
and the seas were destinations of the afterlife.

A billion ripple did come after a zillion perished,
a bunch did reach higher than others, only to fall back
into the pond forgetting each time they don't really matter.

Still each chased the dream of reaching the other shore,
as if they could fly after the accomplishment, none reached,
but even if they did, what does it amount to in the pond-scape!!

Just the ripples over the pond after every rain in this wilderness,
they kept naming themselves, even their emotions, their dreams,
and even their myths, amounting to nothing once the sky was clear,
their names vanished in the stillness of time.
Nothing remains but the Lord.

---

13. Merely a child

O Lord, to whose embrace I want to return,
I am merely a child sent for a swim in this ocean,
and I keep forgetting that the only thing I need ever do
is to return to you as the child who promised to.

If I have played too much on these waves,
if I have been too busy trying to collect the trinkets,
if I have been careless with the other souls,
will you forgive me when I reach back
for nothing frightens me more than
meeting you with a heart of shame.

I keep trying, O Allah, to return to the blissful hug,
but I keep getting into whirlpools and tides and
then into turns and twists of endeavours of the sea,
without ever realizing I wouldn't be here for a moment
if you were not as merciful as you are so perfectly infinite.

Forgive me for all the moments I thought I am alone
for never in the existence have ever you left me
I was merely an ignorant and arrogant soul not yet back.

Clean me from all the leeches that hang on to me and all the -
tentacles that drain me of the last strings of light I hold onto,
my heart was always yours, always there where I left you,
could you remind me of my innocence when I was with you.

---

14. If I go back to me

O the light that shelters all other lights,
O the love that nourishes all the myriad loves,
Can I rest in this bliss for this night,
for I know I would be in pain if I go back to me,
why can I never surpass my forgetfulness?

O the mercy that guides each bird to its grain,
wouldn't you guide this heart to its light, and
remind it that it is nowhere but always in love,
while I keep losing my way and yet another
moment of tears to reach your back to love?

O the care that forgives me and wakes me up now,
wouldn't you forgive the times I forgot and roamed,
wouldn't you erase the images of my mistakes here,
for if you wouldn't who else can ever love me more
to forgive me and to care for an ever-forgetting soul?

---

15. When I fade

In the grief of separation, heart sinks
each moment as I walk through this marsh.
This breath, this walk and this thought,
what are they if not without your love,
O Lord of the eternal bliss and endless mercy,
would you not forgive me for being blinded
in rustles the fake of desires and pursuits?

O the greatness which caused the beauty in
every cadence and throbs inside all that there,
would you not let me come back to you again
and cry to you how much I need you to forgive,
for every other jewel is a fetter for mine heart?

O the grandeur that outshines every dance of -
form and energy in the worlds from ever in time,
would you not let me carry your name in my heart
at that time when I fade from everything in this world
that has ever known me to exist here as a human?

---

16. The peace

Where shall I run to rest, for you are the peace,
to which when one day I would return, O Lord,
for I am an arrogant toddler and even a stray sheep,
could you hold me tighter in your embrace warm
for I am frightened by the lightnings of end of time?

When one day I fall like a dried leaf, pull me into your hug,
O the mercy by which each soul germinates and returns to,
am I too muddied in the sandstorms of desires that wither,
why do I seek anything when all what I perceive is just
other words that would be faded and wiped off morrow?

What in this world is mine when each drop of hue on this -
canvas is from you, nothing to carry nothing to shed, O Lord,
each treasure I shall preserve until you take back from me,
even this vessel, the breath, the dreams and the spouse,
for I never could paint or erase even a dot from this canvas?

How shall I ask forgiveness for the soiled hands these,
like a child rushing to her mother for help, I seek,
could you clean me once again, O the brightest light,
for without you I would remain crying as my eyes are
filled with nothing but ego and pride that I thought I was?

Is it just a nightmare that I slip away from your smile,
will it be a flame that would chain me if I disappointed you,
O kindness, could you let me see your smile for once
before I am awakened to stand trial for my deeds.
wouldn't the waves tell you I tried and failed to float?

Shall I weave a fabric to cover your feet with my tears,
Or shall I remain down with my whispers of remorse,
O forgiveness that I forgot to beseech in my prayers,

wouldn't you consider I am nothing but a grain of sand
stubborn enough to assume the shore is to live till eternity?

What fire or pearls can do to me, O Lord of heavens,
let me forever pray and sing for you, without fear of fire
or desire for wealth of skies, for I seek you the bliss,
where I would be at the feet of the sculptor of worlds,
wouldn't you forgive the dirt I carry to you on my soul?

---

17. I am a tiny fly

I am a tiny fly, confident but foolish,
in tries to open huge doors of this palace,
what am I when I have no wings of my own
and no strength my own except by your love?

I am a tiny spark somewhere in the goldsmith's place,
waiting to declare my existence to the fires and crowns,
forgetting the irony of the thrones that rule this world,
they carry gold but their inner beings in decay.

I am a pond left here to wait for my beloved king,
I reflect the moon and clouds, servant and king,
longing each day to see myself in myself,
O Lord, would you bless me with a shade of bliss?

---

18. To make you proud

To make you proud, O merciful one, I ventured
on this walk, in delusion of the strength of my soul.
As the hue of murky time night percolates deeper
I feel I am helpless even to stay awake this night,
as my desperate hold of your robes gets weakened in
this crowd of my forgetfulness and ignorance.

O ever-forgiving touch to whom I beseech as a child,
hold my hand for I will sink in mud if I am alone here.
Times when I paddle away from the mountain of light ,
let there be a zephyr every time to pull me back to
where my soul is forever anchored prostrated
at the feet of the throne above the worlds that exist.

---

19. Oblivion

Will these tear drops ever suffice to cleanse
my soul of each moment passed in ignorance?
Will these lips ever suffice to take your name,
with all its might and grandeur that it holds?
Will this heart mine ever suffice to love
the love that cares for me even in my oblivion?

Hold me close in your hug, O Allah, for I am
a kid who runs to fire for I think it is sweet.
Accept my imperfect prayers and forgive my soul
for the slave I forget who I am in this play.

20. The play

Irrespective of the lives attached to me,
I find none at times, except for the trust in you,
O Allah, let it be engraved in my every breath
that the only wish that really matters is to
meet you that day with my prayers on the balance.

May the last act of my play be to glorify you,
like no one ever would, and when this vessel
dissolve back into clay, may my soul
still keep listing your hundred names of mercy.

The limited play that I have got to act in this field
the few pains I have to endure on the way to you
the myriad faces I get to ask who their master is,
O Lord, let these each breath help another servant
while one day they meet their master.

21. Not deserving

Not deserving the mercy that was shown to me
in this world where my hands and feet were hidden in dirt,
Not deserving the mercy that I beseech for that day, when
I can be hopeful of only the vastness of your forgiveness.
For you are for the ocean that keeps forgiving me,
my heart is paining in the poisons I have consumed,
would you forgive me again for I am but forgetful as before?

Waves gushing to pull me back in, could I stay in your remembrance
for a night more, for I am afraid of the darkness I have painted
on the beautiful canvas of soul you gave me, what have I done!
O ever-expanse of endless mercy, I am lost in the nightmares of past,
could I stay in your remembrance for a moment more before I leave,
I am afraid would forget again in the whirls of illusions and -mirages?

22. Worldly throngs

Familiar to me are the laughs of worldly throngs,
for I sink and drown in them, the day on these lands,
but are voices of silent prayers to me, for I sleep
even when awake, dead when alive, sad when smile,
I breathe in ignorance and fall in walks, merely to
close a night and open another scroll of moments?

Ya Rabb, may prayers never leave again my lips,
and gratitude never abandon again my tears, as I
keep leaving the pen to draw the words to hold near
my heart when I come to you, with each passing cloud.
May I not leave this shore before leaving hearts
healed from wounds that I caused in folly and foul.

May I not be brought back with the shame of deeds,
for I would be lost if junctures come against, Ya Rabb,
could I rewrite with these words hurriedly my lost times,
for I am desperate for your mercy in any of its shades,
for I am lost in the swarms and swamps again and again.

---

23. My Parents

From that scream of first breath, each moment I meet
leaves me behind like I am meant to be ever-forgotten,
though death arrives closer silently from within veils
like I am meant to neglect the unavoidable visitor.
All this while, you remained with me, O Lord of
all the mirages I wanted to experience in this world, and of
all the mountains of mercy in worlds I was blind about.

You gave me the scents I remember, the sights of world,
everything I ever did receive or perceive in this expanse,
even the gentlest of full moons to walk with me this life, and
gave me this path of your kindest of your mercy to beings,
O the ultimate compassion, I might happen to return just
with nothing but nights of istighfar, and a heart with regret.

If I could see how little grains left in the hour glass for me,
would I have been more careful with the jewels I seek,
would I have sought for your forgiveness more, or would I
still wander this lands forgetting the mercy this life is
O to whom everything submits at this juncture, wouldn't
you accept my forgiveness as I step into your worship.

Your mercy granted me my parents,
for them to be guided I do seek
a strand from the endless thread of
your mercy that holds stars afloat.
O Lord of every breath and presence,
they be shown the sweetness of surrender.

Kind guardians did they be when
I was but a suckling faint breath,
a drop of your mercy did they be when
world could see only the unfortunate.

O Lord you alone are the light of the hearts,
who can guide the hearts and lives
even lost in ever surging whispers.

---

24. O mind

Why aren't you patient, O mind,
till its bright in the woods to see
what's a fruit and what's a foe,
it's still dark and the only fire
to remain near is that of the path?

Why aren't you silent, O mind,
till we are safe on shores of bliss
where only light would remain,
we are still on a floating log in a
violent sea all alone if drowned?

Why aren't you careful, O mind,
when you step into thoughts rogue
that cage you in darkness for nights,
those are just streams that carry
souls straight to abyss of the lost?

Why aren't you surrendered, O mind,
even when I stand before my lord,
why do you wander to unseen days
and unheard applauses, we are still
in the world of wandering mirages?

25. Floods of the signs

Even submerged the floods of the signs,
I kept, Ya Rabb, asking for guidance,
miracle after miracle, answer after another,
still endless treasure your forgiveness,
allowed me exist and protected from
the waves and surges of this world.

If I could ask for another thing more,
could I ask that I be called back
after my voice has reached at least
an ear yearning for guidance, O the light?

---

26. Gust of gratitude

Like the drizzle cleanses the leaves,
could these tears clean this heart I have ignored?
Like the souls are guided to wombs and
lives called back to their grave, carry me
like a leaf in the gust of gratitude.

O existence of mine, what do you still
yearn and cry for when path is discovered?
It's just a matter of patience till our Lord,
keep your tear drops for the most graceful.

O the loci of my search, o the multitude years,
path is reached, now its just patience in each step.
What would I tell my Lord, when I kept forgetting
my way, yet welcomed back with forgiveness?

O the search to burn away dents and dirt
of the mirror that I am somewhere remains,
my Lord is the bestower of truth and wisdom,
what still more you seek, just surrender to him.

---

27. Flames of Infinite Love

What are these wings for, O Lord, except
to rush to your flames of infinite love, before
time runs out to fulfil the promise forgotten?
What are the million shadows and forms of here,
except the signs that talk to soul through heart -
that has long forgotten the silence of surrender?

What are these dreams for, O Lord, except
to yearn to be of use, for your path, in this oyster,
what is surrender if I keep asking for what I desire?
What did the myriad honest guided lights taught
except the grandeur of your love that forgives
even the insidious arrogance in soul mine I carry?

What is the silence of sunrise's hue in east I do see,
except a shadow from a corner of the heavens above
sent as a call to stop dreaming in sleep helplessly?
What are the hundred nights of sleep I indulge in
except a warning that I have to sleep once for long,
would I be afraid to leave forgetting I never arrived?

---

28. Logic and Rules

How could ever truth be caged in logic and rules,
for it is a bird whose feathers are of heaven's tunes?
Could a dream be a dream if not a longing for truth
to a traveller beside the mountains of lost time?

There a few deaths to the souls in love enough for truth,
death when path is met, when path is chosen,
when truth is allowed and when travel begins.
How will I ever be prepared, O Lord of seven beautiful skies?

For I am nothing but lost outside the house of prayers,
could I stay for a few verses more, here as I wait with tears,
what could I ever ask with these lips, when all I ever need
is the forgiveness for carrying this amassed bag of sins?

---

29. How to submit

Life is passing by, O mind, be still,
death is inevitable, O desires, cease,
ink drops dry on paper, scribblings fade,
for gratitude an ocean you still away
trust your heart and weep to the Lord.

Why do you run aimless for time is melting,
what do you chase for you are never owner,
how do you plan for you never see or feel,
let the scroll unfold, be grateful you are.
Life that distracts never halt, but mind can.

Submit the moment for it was never yours,
leave words for eternal love of your soul,
stay here for here is nowhere and no-when,
submit to the be that cast beauty of cosmos,
how to submit when you never cried to Him?

30. Oceans of mercy

How would I thank you for the million colours of the world
if I had no light in eyes, O Lord, same is the state of this heart,
beating and surviving suns and moons, just in dream and breaths,
how would I ever know the infinite love you placed in my soul?

Could I get a peek from the heart-window of this cage and get
a glimpse of the world I belong to, I searched a lot for awakening.
Why to awaken if not to your love, O Lord of the zillion lights,
why to even exist if not for your love and infinite forgiveness?

Could I reach my hand through my wishes to the world of stillness
where the time doesn't flow, where I could be with you forever?
Life is this cycle of separation followed by nights of forgetfulness
and then back before you, for a drop from the oceans of mercy.

---

31. Melt away

Though I yearn to melt away
in the heat of truth's sun morrow,
why do I keep hiding in the borrows
of neglected moments and in crowd,
am I not dear to me or am I just a fool?

Though I dream to cast away for God,
why do I cling to my fears of world still,
why do I postpone meeting the truth,
fake plans and thoughts of treasures
merely to buy me more time in a world
where shadows age and hearts darken?

---

32. Scent of forgetfulness

My prayer to you, O the Creator of the seven skies above,
to hold me near that I wouldn't be carried in the winds
of this desert unknown and scary to me, I seek you O Lord,
I am here to find myself sunk in the sands and crawl up again
in an endless loop of forgetfulness and repentance,
O the mercy that showed me the path to light.

I beg you to erase the dirt I keep gathering in my sleep,
forgive for the times I neglect the love of a million worlds
and to call me back when I have made you proud, O Lord,
let each tear drop of this drenched cloth be a call to you,
let each moment the life in me throbs, be my letter to you.

The dreams and hues that paint these eyes and ears,
let them be filled with your light for that alone is the truth,
let me be called back when I have made you proud,
for if I am not able to, O the Lord that adorned with stars the sky,
please forgive this humble soul for its scent of forgetfulness.

---

33. When my Rabb wishes

When my Rabb wishes, my quest in thirst
shall end like a nightmare that never did visit.
When my Rabb wishes, my days of longing
shall be the past as into bliss of truth I'd step,
O light that guides souls, I am but a little
melting snow heap of tears over the earth.

When my Rabb wishes, I shall be of use,
until then I wait like child left in a house,
did I keep your gifts to me valued enough,
or I forget the universe of love each of those?
Ya Rabb, I am who I am in the mirror of truth,
but you are the ocean of kindness that
let me exist out of nothing but your love.

---

34. All I ever need

O silent breeze, take me away from the fake noises,
to the land where you gently tap the mountains to
lull the birds in the bosoms of night. Take me away
to the time where you would wait for the clouds to sleep
to wake the white blossom in the cool river of sky.

O doors of the hut I am hallucinating to own,
from the songs of men and women shut me off,
from them for the song I seek can't ever be heard,
let me remain in this silence for the one I pray to
is the forgiveness that guides the lost tunes.

O heavens in the mind that I create in vain,
could you ever imagine the love the Master holds
to sustain each sparkle and glitter of the universe?
Why am I dragged to the swamps of music of world,
when even a handful of his names is all that I ever need?

---

35. I am found again

I cried for things that I wished for,
but never cried the same for you yet.
I kept spending away time in words
forgetting the what I seek is waiting
with love of a million worlds in silence.

I walked for dreams that I cared for,
never long enough on the straight path,
may be 'cause the coward me knows
in glaring light of truth, no thing remains.

O the mercy that gently glides a bird's feather,
O the kindness that the wings trust in each flight,
I am sadly an actor just playing to be truthful,
You are the gentleness that made this world,
won't you give me a day where I am found again?

---

36. A weak glimmer

What am I running away from,
for I am a frightened soul in this dark room?
I sleep through dawn lights merely to -
realize am just a weak glimmer without you.
When I ever been except under shade of love,
even as I hide in this dark room to have
a shadow of my own for that these acts,
just a glimmer weakening away from you?

Whatever I would be, I already ever am,
for my heart's smile is when with you,
will you accept me back under shade of love,
if I return as the faintest glimmer from this room?
Why am I so afraid to step out to spring's sky,
for I never belonged to the room anyway,
I been but a flute with forgotten tunes,
would I be singing for you ever again?

37. I thought

In my arrogance I thought I search,
when have I ever traversed anywhere
except that you allowed path to shrink,
still arrogant the foolish mind of mine
thinks I am the one who walks with torch.

In my sleep I thought I am the seeker,
when have I ever sought anything
except in me that you placed love for it,
still sleeping the delusional mind of mine
thinks I am the one to seek on this path.

In my forgetfulness I thought you are far,
when have I ever for a second existed
except that hugged by your love for me,
still forgetful the careless mind of mine
thinks you are the one to be reached afar.

---

38. Impatient child

Like an impatient child crying for sweets,
I keep crying for unveiling truth in mirror,
O Lord of all lights and forms, you are the
giver of everything that ever to reach me,
You alone is my master whom I cry to,
may this traveller me be steadfast
on the miles to be travelled on truth.

Like a child with ever-changing wishes,
I keep asking for new glitters that I dream,
O Lord of all dreams and souls, you are the
giver of all love that I have ever held in heart,
You alone is my guide whom I seek from,
may this bag of dreams be guided
on the one path that ever leads to you.

---

39. Before again

The dusty misused vase the heart -
I surrender. Hope it's filled with love
before I am distracted again back
to the ever-dancing shadows of here,
O Lord of all knowledge and unknowns,
forgive me for not being awake enough.

The rusty words used but little for you -
I surrender. Hope it's guided with bliss
before I am dragged again back there
to the actors' play of mere world here,
O Lord of all strengths and hearts,
forgive me for not repenting enough.

The heavy sack of swollen remorse-
I surrender. Hope it's accepted from me,
before I walk again to the field of mirk
of loops of sins again unstopped,
O Lord of all events, scenes and futures,
forgive me for not being yours enough.

---

40. When I return

If my soul is taken between words I scribble,
Ya Allah, let it be healed in your love
though I chose the cage to be forgotten,
it's you that could guide me in the dark and
it's your greatness this fool keeps denying,
forgive me, O Lord of all the lights of skies.

If my heart reaches its time as I sleep,
Ya Rabb, let it be with a final prayer to you
in this form of forgetfulness and sins,
for when I return before you with repentance
it's just your greatness this soul ever prays to,
forgive me, O Lord of all the love in worlds.

---

41. My soul

The drops sliding through leaves to earth,
could you remind me again and again to repent,
for in forgetfulness I keep finding myself lost,
you know, my master, how much I need you.

Let my tears not stop when I stop uttering your name,
Let my tears flood when I call to you in silence of night,
Let my heart crumble when in me doubt is placed,
Let my soul be called to return when you are proud of me.

---

42. Like a child

Like a child staying away to save his sleep
from door that opens to the room of light,
how funny flying to lands unseen is the mind
when I call to the path my heart belongs.

Like a child making excuses to play more
in the garden familiar now to eyes and feet,
how funny hanging to thoughts is the mind
when I realize I forgot again to be reminded.

Like a child crying for the toy snatched away
from hands that got used to its magic tricks,
how funny lamenting over lost time is the mind
when all I ever have is now that I am not yet in.

43. Pull me from the flames

Pull me from the flames away
when habits do pull me again,
I am a fly here to live just a day
let me not die except for you,
for I am in chains of me and mine,
free me, O Lord, to the truth high.

Pull me from the flames away
when my me get cunning again,
I am a lute here to play for you,
when tune does float finally that day
let me useful to this garden's souls,
shade me, O Lord, from rain of lies.

---

44. What could I know

They say about the wide opened gates
that we could just walk out if with care,
O Lord, what could I know about those
when fear mine is if I ever would wake
for heavy is heart in search of my light,
they say it's a choice not to see.

They say about the rivers that flow,
that we could just flow to you if with love,
O Lord, what could I know about those
when fear mine is if I ever would know
the sweetness of this path I was blessed,
they say it's a choice not to walk.

They say about the trees that grow
in heavens with every your name if told,
O Lord, what could I know about those
when fear mine is if I ever would flow
to lands where I am one with my prayer,
they say it's a choice not to know.

---

45. Forever

As they leave the clouds, do raindrops fear,
sucked out of their crowd to join the sea?
For parting from heights of sky, do they cry,
or for meeting beloved sea they rejoice?

To the dark chandelier huge, do they cling,
or to the will of the eternal love, they submit?
However far they travel, do they regret,
time they reach their home forever more?

Whatever dreams they carried, do they care,
once they are back in million droplet hugs?
When that day I return to my home, will I fear,
out of this vessel, forever to be in love?

---

46. Back to my thoughts

How many nights for this seed to sprout,
as it waits for the cool kiss of the sky above?
How many days for this mind to be still,
as it waits for the warm hug of silence within?

How many washes for this vessel to be clean
as I struggle to clean in the dusk of the day?
How many verses for this soul to be awake
as it sleeps through noons and nights crying?

How many dreams for the nights to be calm
as I walk with a mind like storm-wrapped sea?
How many times before the time is still
as I sink in your love to be awakened to you?

How many woods and mountains to walk still
as I search for the truth with a hurting heart?
How many moments for the moments of bliss
as I am helplessly again back to my thoughts?

---

47. Like an infant

Like an infant about the people around,
I am jealous of the ones you love more,
for they know to walk as I struggle to stand,
can I be lifted up I am desperate to see sky?

Like a bird stranded in the desert of life,
without ever knowing when it would rain,
only if I knew how to fly as I struggle to stand,
can I be guided to the bliss of hidden silence?

Like those lands revealed in lightning at night,
will there be a time where i just be here
in submission to glory that I can't fathom,
O the light hidden in existence of each moment?

---

48. I hide

When I drape myself in acts of selflessness,
I hide my selfish me where only you can see,
I want to be in love as breath follows another
and when breath is just but once past for me.

When I cower in fear of leaving your house again,
I hide my tear drops where only you can reach,
I want to be in submission to you as I walk,
whether it is over mud or thorns, light or dark.

When I feel shame for wishing for things other than you,
I hide my words written for you where only you live,
I want to dissolve every drop of my soul in your love,
and when I return, repent to you with all that I carry.

---

49. Who will but you

Not knowing what to expect outside my sleep,
I keep clinging to the ever changing scripts of my dreams.
O Lord, who will but you can shake me from
the depths of the prison I create for myself.

My mind keeps changing its shades and smells,
My body keeps changing with each grain in hourglass,
O Lord, who will but you can wake me from
the nightmare of never waking up to your love.

Not smelling the fragrance of your kindness,
I keep twisting and turning in my bed of futile desires,
O Lord, who will but you can love this poor soul
even after being such a hopeless student.

My hands keep being dragged to tasks of morrows,
breaths keep being continued from one sunrise to another,
O Lord, who will but you can bring silence to this hideously
clanging vessel that is lost somewhere in the dark

50. Let me pass this night

Let me pass this night in tears,
for I never asked enough for the truth,
for if I ever did, I would have known
the sweetness they know of prayers
who carry those verses in their hearts.

Let me pass this night in here, alone,
without wishes for heights that are low,
for everything I ever have asked for
never meant to be carried in my soul,
for you, O Lord, are the highest of all.

Let me pass this night now and more,
without ever thinking I am poor in wealth,
for what greater treasure to carry in this life
than longing for steadfastness on the path,
for nothing else is cure to a sleeping heart.

Let me pass this night away from desires
for pleasures are bound to cease on death,
except that which is blessed with your name,
O Lord, I am but a poet without enough words.

---

51. Peace be upon you

Peace be upon you,
O whose smiles adorned sunsets of Madinah,
Peace be upon you,
O whose mercy is itself an ocean to thank for.
Peace be upon you,
for whom trees competed to shade,
and clouds rushed near to wish peace.
Peace be upon you,
for whom moon lit brighter just for
a glimpse of its reflection on your face.

A new world revealed in each colour of light that falls,
a new shade of your love overflowing for your nation
each moment that met you on the walk here of life.
Each moment that you were oasis we rushed to,
left a tale of the highest way for breaths we take.

---

52. Refusing to submit

O Lord, forgive this seed for being sleeping me,
grant growth into a tree shading your lovers,
grant fruits for the children passing by.
World would whirl again and again the same,
day and night would wrap earth with seasons,
O Lord, forgive me for being a sleeping seed,
forgive for tendencies these of my heart
still refusing to submit to your love so grand.

O Lord, forgive this light the selfish it is a fool lost,
in silence, addicted to thoughts, instead of prayers.
Time again leaves the now abandoned in the past
snatching away a breath of opportunity to submit,
O Lord, forgive me for being careless on your path,
forgive for the oceans of wasted words and actions,
forgive the soul still refusing to submit with everything.

53. How scared should I be

What am I selling each day in my slumber clad in perfume,
am I selling words I collect each hour for travellers' smiles,
Or am I just selling lies to snatch the meal for tonight,
what do I own to sell in this world market of time?

Do I carry kindness for travellers gullible and weak,
when carelessly chatting away the lies to sell trinkets,
how scared should I be to fool a soul submitted to Him
for He sustains all time-bound and beyond afar and near?

Am I a farmer who nurtures or am I a cruel tyrant mad,
when walking this path in sleep careless and distracted,
how scared should I be to mock at a soul walking to Him,
for His love allows thunders to roar and clouds to float?

---

54. Time doesn't care

Time doesn't care about my hesitation to start,
night doesn't care about my ideas of journey's end.
The images and dreams I made of journey must go,
for I just stare at path without even a single step taken.
Self was never meant to know anything still caged in world
it was His mercy to me that brought me now here.

If I wait for my feathers to fall, I may not fly,
If I wait for sun to be higher, I may not start,
what do I wait still when I have waited enough for this,
It's just a plunge in submission and forever inside bliss.
O my soul, what do you wait for when you are in pangs of love,
let's surrender our names and memories for we never owned.

If I wait for the silence to wrap windy night,
If I wait for the moon to be brighter behind clouds.
What if I am again back in pond of mirages to be lost,
as that's where most of me still wants to be forgotten.
O my soul, what do you wait for when you are wiser of us,
let's surrender our forms and colours to be by us found.

---

55. What would the world say

What name would the world give to me,
world where robes, music and appeal,
taken as reflection of what hides within?
What would world say about my love for you,
for they boasts of truth behind all the veils?
I am a traveller in devotion to you not to them.

When thrones more important than lives,
what world did we humans nurture, O Lord,
they think only rulers would be asked of these?
When would the world feed the starving poor,
what is saved as souls left to die in groups?
All does have the same earth to call home.

---

56. I now

Memory juggling mind and image obsessed intellect
do have a quarrel in me as who best at imprisoning
the being in me that wants to rise above the clouds.
Even fears and wishes to submit so that bridge is crossed,
for it is His everything everywhere, self His mere slave.

What am I now except for a pile of memories
and theories I gathered and put together layers of?
What am I now except for a forgotten tune
yearning to be used in worship of his Lord?

Where the forge of scenes and talks is in mind
there is a child who is afraid to be silent still,
how to tell it even death and existence is but
by my Lord's mercy that I keep forgetting about?

___

57. But you are

I am here but not yet here, in pursuits futile,
but you are eternally here though I can't see.
Between each breath, the fool self chooses
the world of mirages and movements, again.
Between the each heartbeat of a seeker's heart,
the childish self chooses to day-dream than perceive.

I am trying but still hiding behind selfish questions,
but you are eternally the answer though I keep asking.
Between prayers, the distracted breath chooses
the world of competition and worries, again.
Between each throb of the universe's beat,
the desire-filled self chooses to fall into the flood.

I am a slave awake to demands of world,
but not to the loving master who chooses me.
Between each thought, I choose to think,
though, if not that, I could be before you.
Between each bubble burst of transient time,
the unaware self chooses to sink in ambitions.

---

58. Submission alone

Near the flame of prayers, the stone heart melts,
within pages of this book, tear drops find abode,
In loneliness, the self fights the beasts of thoughts,
O fragrant traveller, in submission alone all of answers.

Wax melts and again fed, till there is nothing but flame,
I am but a fly away afar in the valley of questions,
looking at the oceans and anxious how to cross,
O wandering soul, in submission alone is the travel's bliss.

Wings are burnt anyway in separation from truth,
I am but a nameless leaf always in mercy's shade,
I may cling on or shed, green or dry, happy or sad,
O lurking doubts, through submission alone is land of lights.

---

59. Silent Walk

Even in the brightest light, dusty pages hard to read,
even in the calmest of nights, a seeker's sleep disturbed,
even the clearest of water drops find itself in clay pot,
keep walking for the path is straight but weak your eyes.

Even in the heaviest of rain, if path is my shade,
even in the loudest of thunders, if my heart recites,
I have started lighting the room with tiny flames,
alone is the wait and together is this silent walk.

60. Can it ever

The brook that reflects the grand forest,
can it ever contain the songs a bird sings?
The sky in which the clouds float smoothly,
can it ever draw the images a child dreams?

The bubble that lenses the world around it,
can it forever keep treasuring its breath as it floats?
The lullaby that the sleepy baby hears in her cradle,
can it ever fully say the love that the mother is?

When I am called back before you, O Lord,
I would witness the grandeur of love and mercy,
of which only a drop I can realize from this speck.

---

61. Who could

Who could give louder an invitation to the path today,
than the beautiful skies above of night and day?
Both in their grandeur trying to paint the majesty and mercy
of the creator whose is all that is there ever to exist?

Who could recite a poem louder in your name than
the flocks of birds, rustling leaves and whispering winds?
O Lord, let the words that find themselves in these thoughts,
be of those to call back a heart long away and lost.

Forgiveness boundless that allowed water to my soul,
O Lord, let the words that I once gathered from this world
find themselves offered thay they bring blissful tears
in hearts who build caves of ignorance just like I once.

---

62. Aim

What should the devotee tree aim to be, is it
of prayer beads that a vessel carries in hands
while the soul spends hours in remembrance,
or is it the house that shades a family of light,
through all rain and sun, cries and laughs?

What should the drops of rain aim to be, is it
to be with thirsty child on street barren there,
or is it a cup of drops that a righteous use to
clean their face in the name of the Lord?

Is there an aim too low or too high for the surrenderer,
is there a life less or more in the sight of our Lord,
when submitted, aims merely a preparation game
for the day you would call souls to this path.

---

63. Forgetting that

I kept collecting mirrors from ones I met on walk,
in hopes one day I could see a beautiful me,
forgetting that each did have only the distorted ones,
as the true me is in the reflection of a slave on sea of love.

Each juncture I collected a name of you from others,
in hopes of completing your image in all its glory,
forgetting that each did have only a part of each name,
as your names are beyond thought vessels to hold.

---

64. Not mine

Covered in the slimy mud of ego and desires,
I reach out to the depths for a gentle touch.
I kept thinking I am here to live, this fool,
failed to notice I was brought here as a boon.
What do I surrender when even my mind is not mine?
What do I still desire when even this me is not here?

I am being dragged into world of duties,
endless seems the roles this actor must take,
but with your grace, may I witness this me
offering my every moment on your feet
at the service of this creation dream.

I hope that one day I can be near you,
words and wishes washed away
with tears of joy. I would stand before you
silently enjoying the love you always are.

---

65. Brightest of full moons

Centuries away from you, peace be upon you,
still walking in the light you carried of the path,
O the brightest of full moons that wept for us,
I am ashamed for not praying for siblings enough.

When the thrones and crowns are mere tools to divide us,
In Rabb alone, as you taught, do we place our trust.
Muslims frightened by muslims, Islam hidden by force,
who could unite us than the Lord of all hearts.

When we are among trials to our siblings,
O the one who carries us in your prayers,
as you taught, we stay steadfast in this path,
even if we are of the ever-misfits they say.

66. In search

In search of peace, I knocked on doors,
giving them smiles and asking them to let
me breathe in peace, forgetful as usual
you alone the ever-giving source of peace.

In search of peace, I planned for mountains,
painting the pictures so bright in my mind
to latch on to the plan, forgetful as usual
you alone the spring of peace I ever need.

In search of peace, I push my being to alone,
attempting to clear the clogged thoughts,
to have a drop of silence, forgetful as usual
you alone the source and destination of stillness.

---

67. Who am I

Who am I to verify, realize, prove or argue, I am
mere a seeker who knows not what is sought.
In search of missing pieces, I travelled in time
ageing each day, desperately in pursuit of the truth.

Who am I to seek, gather, find or describe, I am
mere a poor soul in existence from your love.
In preparation of me returning to you, I kept
composing my truth forgetting you are the truth.

Who am I to rule, beg, collect or share, I am
mere a transient colour drop in this canvas of yours.
My presence fading from canvas since birth,
I wish never to be of the ungrateful colours, O Lord.

---

68. Here is a dream

I don't pray to be a sculptor of words and poems
but I wish to be a poem in submission to you, ya Allah,
I don't pray to be a scholar carrying light for mankind
but I wish to be a light of love for all that you love.

When the moon's glory is replaced by the rising sun,
summon this heart to silence for I belong to you.
When tiny stars get their turn to adorn the sky,
summon this slave to prayer for you are my master.

When the mind mine is deep in sleep at night,
remind this ignorant child that all of here is a dream.
When the days turn into years in the rustle of a leaf,
remind this distracted to pray more, for the act could end.

---

69. Drop from the oceans

In your hands a fluttering butterfly is allowed to fly,
in your love angels decent with tranquillity upon hearts,
Ya Allah, could I be given the veiled drink of truth,
tired of this repetitive game of emotions, I cry to you.

In your mercy water quenches the thirst of the drinker,
in your mercy may the fire of ignorance never touch me,
Ya Allah, please open my heart to the truth I shy away from,
tired of my arrogance and its forms varied, I cry to you.

In your blessing the stars adorn the sky and clouds move,
in your endless compassion, the heart of every atom exists to be,
Ya Rabb, please give light to the eyes of my heart
so that I do always witness your glory in each moment.

In your wisdom, we are made aware of what we will ever know,
In your beneficence each flower that blooms get its chance,
Ya Jabbar, please fill to the brim of my heart love for you
so that I could exist merely to spread a drop from the oceans.

---

70. Among us

The ones who can see among us, Ya Allah,
use us to show to the sleeping world those tyrants
that keep torturing the oppressed poor.
The ones who can speak among us, Ya Allah,
allow us to be the voice of all children
who are thrown away to starve and die.

The ones who can read among us, Ya Allah,
allow us the fountains of wisdom to treasure
the most glorious among all paths you sent.
The ones who can write among us, Ya Allah,
use us as vehicles to be strength and words
of every beloved soul oppressed and hidden away.

71. Rules and rights

Rules and rights, speeches painted about the path.
Merely love and love I witness in the path, O Lord,
your limitless love that floods the worlds all where,
guide me to this soul's peak to be the prayer here.
I am forever a mere servant of yours, can I ask for
souls on the path to be guided and forgiven always.

If I am the sand on the dune, let me never be
one to rage over the tents of believers, O Lord.
If I am a piece of soil where your beloved souls rest
use me as a tool to give your love even to the dead.
Use me, O Lord, like a rain or light or a flower or a tree.

Debates rage to seek the best of the ones on path.
I am forever a mere servant of yours, can I ask for
the path to be fragrant again by hearts that can love.

---

72. Breeze of peace

The world rejoices at chance each to defame the path of truth,
O muslim, my dua is that your heart be overpoured with love
till you have no choice but to share the love with passers-by.

May we be like fragments of mirror
competing to reflect the grandeur
of the brightest ever of full moons
to adorn the most beautiful Madinah.

May we be the courage and wisdom of this age,
world will always watch for we are misfits loud,
unwilling to be programmed and tamed,
holding till death to the best of the ways revealed to us.

When darkness and its slaves sew stories and songs
against our children and the old, they forget we exist
to spread love and peace, in a world with values sacrificed,
we exist to be the breeze of peace to the world lost in greed.

---

73. O world who cannot

O world who cannot hear pain,
are homeless mere criminals for losing out in the
games greedy of the engines gluttonous you made?
O world who cannot see hearts,
are the poor disgusting to touch for you just because
they couldn't afford the masks you wear of fake?

O world who cannot cry for another helpless soul,
heartbeat of a poor is as loud as a sky of thunders,
fear for we have failed if they are outside on cold nights -
merely for we were greedy to steal their rights.

O world who is addicted to rules of useless games,
how much should we make building a roof restricted
merely so that afford some can and some cannot,
fear the Lord, as a generation, for we have failed.

---

74. O believer

For atheists can never make you dance, O believer,
an outsider to the kingdoms of world, you will ever be.
For greed and rewards cannot entice you,
a stranger to the ever changing times, you will ever be.

For you carry heavens in your heart, O believer,
a mere rebel to the chains of the fake, you will ever be.
For you are the love and peace to many forgotten,
through you may the eternal love flow to millions more.

---

75. When all it matters

One lifetime each of many spent looking at the stars,
one lifetime each of many spent fighting over stones,
in the end, another lifetime spent counting the corpses instead of
stars.

Why does it matter how burdened with stones our hands,
when all it matters is only a little, we can feed ourselves?
Why does it matter how much we carry in our carts,
when nowhere much we can travel heavy?

Why does it matter who all sit in the thrones,
when all it matters is if sun rises morrow?
Why does it matter who all shine among us,
when all it matters is that everyone fades?

Why does it matter if a leaf or mountain forms our roof,
when all that matters is helplessness when asleep?
Why does it matter if alone or engulfed in acquaintances,
when all that matters is the journey within in this life?

---

76. My image

With myriad corrections, on this rock,
I keep sculpting my image, thinking,
I would be happy when I have finished.
I wonder, which me I love more,
the one that resides within this body,
or the one somewhere inside this rock?

When someone sees me on the streets,
who do they disapprove, the one in me,
or the one inside the mirror, my shadow?
why does anyone want to argue,
for nobody knows a thing, just weighing
their bundle of ignorance against the world?

---

77. Final flicker

When I am at the final flicker of life here,
Ya Rabbi, could mine flame be turned to a wildfire
to engulf in my humble love all that you love?
When I am at the final prostration of dream here,
Ya Rabbi, could mine prayer be for all who souls
have walked and will walk this of paths the glorious.

When I am at the final choice of how to be,
Ya Allah, could mine choice be to seek forgiveness
for I have been a forgetful soul again and again?
When I am at the final door of moments here,
Ya Allah, could mine everything be in submission
to you alone, O the one to whom I shall return?

78. I do pray

When the truth that all has to taste visits me,
O Lord, let the path I was shown come to my aid
to allow me to thank you for all the forgiveness,
to say for one last time that I believe in your mercy.

I do pray that my desires, pursuits, and wishes,
all left behind, I'd still call out to you from depths of this-
being, who has drenched in showers of your love, I'd-
thank for the light I was guided to only by your mercy.

I do pray that I be not scared, for the fearful soul I always was,
like once I came to this dream, I have to leave the familiar behind.
Let me be given strength for a final moment in your prayer,
this slave could never tell you how much a perfect master you are.

I do pray that my sins unknown is left hidden in your mercy,
my mere handful of deeds grown by your love, my soul aware.
As I leave this dream, could I leave some of my words here
so that I could still love millions of siblings on this beloved path?

I do pray that tales of my arrogance and greed cease
to exist the moment I consume last grain of my hour glass,
let these words be my apology to all of forms and beings
I would have transgressed from my bubble in my ignorance.

---

79. If you manage

O reader, if you manage to cross the familiar,
let me know of how sweet the nectar.
I am just a poet scribbling about unknown,
but I will keep a share for you if
I ever am found in limitless love beyond.

O seeker, if you manage to witness the certainty,
let me know how flooded in tears your room.
I am just a child asking for the largest gift,
but I will keep a piece of my ecstasy if
I ever am found in the undeniable so perfect.

O traveller, if you manage to submit just to Him,
let me know how you surrendered even your fears.
I am just a man trying to walk faster in this dream,
but I will keep waiting for you there if by His mercy,
I ever manage to wake up from this cage.

Notes

Notes

Notes

Printed in Great Britain
by Amazon

40796801R00057